Grandmama,
I hope you enjoy!
Can't wait to read
your book!! :)

Love Always

integration

AN OPEN-AT-RANDOM BOOK OF THOUGHT-PROVOKING LYRICS AND IMAGES

integration

An Open-at-Random Book of Thought-Provoking Lyrics and Images

Kellee Maize

Photography by Laura Petrilla
Paintings by Octeel (Matthew R Macri)

PITTSBURGH

Integration

Copyright 2012 by Kellee Maize

ISBN-13: 978-0-9832726-7-0

Library of Congress Control Number: 2001012345
CIP information available upon request

First Edition, 2012

St. Lynn's Press . POB 18680 . Pittsburgh, PA 15236
412.466.0790 . www.stlynnspress.com

Book design–Brooke Schooles
Editor–Catherine Dees

Photography © Laura Petrilla
Paintings © Octeel (Matthew R Macri)

Printed in The United States of America on FSC recycled paper using vegetable-based inks.

This title and all of St. Lynn's Press books may be purchased for educational, business, or sales promotional use. For information please write:
Special Markets Department . St. Lynn's Press . POB 18680 . Pittsburgh, PA 15236

10 9 8 7 6 5 4 3 2 1

This book is dedicated to someone who is not yet
born at the date of writing this. Little Gyan or Freya,
your mom and dad put so much love into this book and
they are my family, so you are too. I understand you are
bringing forth protective spider energy and unconditional
love. I hope that this book can be a reflection of your
perfection and create the kind of joy and light
that you are bringing to us.

I loved you before you arrived. xoxo

introduction

When St. Lynn's Press approached me about writing this book I fell into what you might call a moment of awe. I had always fantasized about writing a book someday, and the idea of creating an open-at-random book of my song lyrics struck a chord, because it reminded me of some of the inspirational practices I do in my life and find very valuable.

For years I have "pulled cards" at random for inspiration and guidance. I started playing with Tarot, but more often I use my increasing collection of oracle, goddess, angel or animal cards. These cards always speak to me and when I considered the idea of a book that may potentially have a similar effect and was using my lyrics, I was in! I trusted that this was put in my path for a reason.

In this book you will find excerpts from four of my albums:
    Age of Feminine (2007)
    Aligned Archetype (2010)
    Integration (11/11/11)
    Owl Time (scheduled for release 12/12/12)

I make music because I want to share ideas, experiences and concepts that have in some way elevated my consciousness and opened my eyes, heart and mind. I know not everyone can relate to the way I deliver it in my music, so I am *so* grateful to you for having interest in our book, and I hope that you may draw something of value from it. This is not like the cards I use regularly because the lyrics were not written to answer a question, but my intention is that the universe will speak to you somehow through these pages, the way the cards speak to me.

I always love involving my soul family in projects and I immediately thought about my dear friends Matt and Laura, as their work very much aligns with my worldview. They are not only fabulous friends, but incredibly talented and insightful artists. For a long time I have been wanting to do something bigger with them. I also asked my many-talented friend Brooke to design the book. St. Lynn's was gracious enough to allow us to collaborate! As you open these pages you will see Laura's and Matt's beautiful images paired with my lyrics – a multi-sensory sharing, from our hearts to yours.

Sending you peace, love and light always!

I honor each of you
For all your darkness and your light
And the integration can now begin, this night

TIME TRAVEL INTO A NEW PORTAL
WE ALL SHALL ENTER, THE CITY OF STEEL HOLDS A KEY
TO TRANSFORMATION IN ITS FOURTH RIVER
I HAVE NO DOUBT YOU ALL WILL GATHER
FEMININE ENERGY RETURNS
LINKING US TO THE HIGHER CONSCIOUSNESS
YOU HAD AT BIRTH BEFORE YOU WERE DOMESTICATED
IT IS, AS WAS PREDICTED BY ALL INDIGENOUS PEOPLES
THE TIME IS NOW
AFFIRM YOUR DREAMS FOR YOURSELF AND THIS PLANET
WHEN YOU SEE 11:11 ON OUR TIMEKEEPERS
IT IS NOT ABOUT WISHING, IT IS ABOUT CREATING
TIME IS NOT REAL
WE ARE OF ONE UNIVERSAL BODY
YOU CREATE YOUR REALITY AND PEACE IS REVOLUTION
KNOW, NOW, THE WORLD IS IN YOU
WHAT, FRIENDS, SHALL YOU DO WITH THIS WISDOM?
FIND YOUR INNER CHILD
RELEASE YOUR STRUGGLE
LOVE EVERYONE AND EVERYTHING
BE THE CHANGE YOU WISH TO SEE
TELL ME NOW, YOU KNOW, THERE IS ANOTHER
SPACE TIME REALITY
WHERE YOU CAN MAKE A HEAVEN
11:11

*Eleven 11, **Aligned Archetype***

As the ocean floor becomes oil slicks
I think this is the basis
For unplugging the matrix
I could see it in our faces

Trapped, **Integration**

Time to go to dynamic from the static

While the women walk miles to get water

And they're leading all the sheep to the slaughter

Mother earth is getting hotter we forgot her

And now she's pissed and igniting her daughters

Mad Humans, **Integration**

I often undulate, try to dominate
And my ego taking over, ain't no time to waste
I ask for a guide who in I confide
Tell 'em homey can U help me, I can not decide
If this is what i want, if this is why I'm here
If I am driven only by all my concern and fear
And then I open up and I can find the joy
Reachin' deep inside my being, let my heart deploy

*Listen, **Owl Time***

But this is all made up of words

That we've given meaning

And someone else said it's true

It's all perception, we created this doom

But we got that kinda power in this hour

Why not devour our bullshit

The Fact Is, Integration

THE CLOCK IS ALMOST THERE
LINEAR TIME IS ENDING
NO SENSE IN BEING SCARED
POSITIVE VIBES NEED SENDING

*Evolve, **Aligned Archetype***

97 % of our DNA is
unexplained by science
They call it junk
A caterpillar and a butterfly
have got the same DNA
Now tell me can
you feel that funk

Flying Caterpillar, Owl Time

He was the sunshine, She was the night
A perfect balance of darkness and light,

Despite the difference you know that They Will Keep it goin' thru every evening and every day

Katy's Song, ***Wedding Song***

u can feel the feminine vibration
and the presence of the spaceships
interdimensional stations
hurry hurry, they are waiting

*The Fact Is, **Integration***

A samurai that's still ticklish

Catch Me, **Integration**

I HAD TO FACE
MY DEMONS
SO I WILL NOT
BE THEM
TO MOTHER EARTH I FREED THEM, TRANSMUTE THEM

AND COMPLETE THEM

*Shadow, **Integration***

hopi prophecy, nostradamus wrote it see

it's our duty to return the mother to the tree

water the root, it's an emergency

age of aquarius, bring them water, set them free

you are the light
you are the god
you are the way
other than in name

and love is
much more
important
than fame

Free Up, **Owl Time**

Indigenous people
They knew this all along
We bowed to cash and steeple
Consumers doing wrong
But you can feel it now
Life is yours to create
Your heart can heal and wow
If you just concentrate

Evolve, **Aligned Archetype**

LOVE YOUR ENEMY
OR BE THEIR SLAVE
BE THE CHANGE
WE WANNA SEE
OR DIG OUR GRAVE

IF LIFE IS A GAME
HOW WE
GONNA PLAY

Divine, **Integration**

WE'RE AT THE DAWN OF A WHOLE NEW AGE
CLOSING THE BOOK 'N I'M RIPPIN' THE PAGE
TO SEE A NEW LIFE WE ALL MUST ENGAGE
ON THIS NEW EARTH I AM TAKING THE STAGE
STEERING THE SHIP, I AM BEHIND THE WHEEL
I CAN CREATE IT AND I'LL MAKE IT REAL
NO NEED TO HATE IT, FEAR IT OR STEAL
YOUR BRAIN DETERMINES JUST HOW YOU FEEL
THEN HOW YOU FEEL AFFECTS HOW YOU ACT
BAD BEHAVIOR, THEN YOU'RE OFF TRACK
POSITIVE THINKING IS WHAT YOU LACK
THOUGHT BECOMES THING, YOU BEST BELIEVE THAT

Thought to Thing, **Aligned Archetype**

WE CREATE OUR OWN, OUR OWN REALITY
EVERYTHING IN THE WORLD IS A REFLECTION OF THE ME
USE YOUR ENERGY FOR SOMETHING NEW, UN-THOUGHT
DO WHAT YOU ALWAYS DID YOU'LL GET WHAT YOU ALWAYS GOT

Hasta Abajo, **Integration**

WE ALREADY ARE PSYCHICALLY IN TUNE TO THE STARS

Tree of Life, **Owl Time**

MY TRANSCENDENCE WAS DEPENDENT ON LOOKIN' AT YOU WITH A REVERENCE THAT I SHOULD LOOK AT MYSELF WITH

*La La Love, **Integration***

Find me flyin' high
        to a different world

I am more than a girl
        the sand became a pearl

And now I'm floatin' in the sea
        changing out of a me

To universality become another entity

Ascend, I commend you
        pretendin' is no longer true

No end, no start and no attaching glue

Do you hear me, are you weary?

Are you sick of this, of all the trickery?
We worry, we hurry
        we're afraid we're dirty

        We're guilty, we're scared
                look bad - don't dare!

Divine, **Integration**

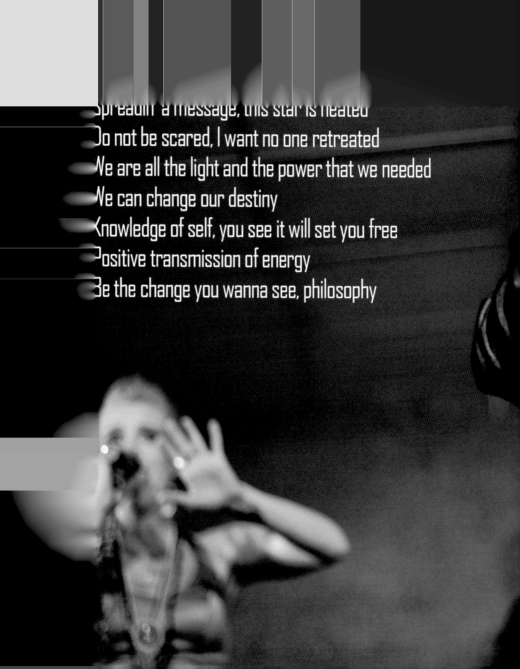

Spreadin' a message, this star is heated
Do not be scared, I want no one retreated
We are all the light and the power that we needed
We can change our destiny
Knowledge of self, you see it will set you free
Positive transmission of energy
Be the change you wanna see, philosophy

*Pulse, **Aligned Archetype***

Inside your right brain
This is a new plane
Of existence
You heard the mystics
Feminine return
No more on stakes burn
The mother's waiting
Her ground is breaking
She will make new seeds
Boys 'n girls, 5th breed
Out of dimension
Time will be questioned
All new invention
Universe extension

Eleven 11, *Aligned Archetype*

TOO MANY KIDS DEAD OR AIN'T BEEN FED TOO MANY INDIGENOUS HAVE BLED YEAH WE'RE PUTTING THE PATRIARCHY TO BED THE ONE OUTSIDE AND INSIDE OUR HEAD WE PLANNED IT ALL WE'VE MADE OUR OWN BED TIME TO AWAKE, EVOLVE AND DEFEND

Mad Humans, *Integration*

Friday Night Flu, *Aligned Archetype*

DO YOU KNOW THAT YOU'RE LUCKY?
YOU HAVE FOOD TO EAT
DO YOU KNOW THAT YOU'RE LUCKY?
THERE ARE SHOES UPON YOUR FEET

Freakuency, *Aligned Archetype*

PROTECT US FROM PSYCHIC ATTACK
THE ODDS AGAINST US CANNOT STACK
IF EVERYONE HAS EVERY BACK
LACK OF RESPECT

IS REALLY WACK

*Mothership, **Aligned Archetype***

identities thick as forests before we cut the trees

droppin' on our knees

needing a savior like Jesus

lust, greed, hate, these are us

we must

breathe fate

into existence, we are the mystics

that could fix this

this is it.

*Divine, **Integration***

The polar sides they separate
Negative waits at positive's gates
The magnet's growing now clear the slate
Empty your mind now so much at stake
Turn off the news you know it's all fake
Inside your brain disastrous quake
Powers inside of all of us to make
A heaven now for our children's sake

Start None, **Aligned Archetype**

I will insinuate
communicate and elevate
Until everyone has freedom
they could celebrate

L`Outro, **Integration**

Finally the earth's come
around, use a new part
of your brain, make a
new sound

All we want is love, it's
making our hearts
pound

The new children are

here, they are coming

out the ground

Third Eye, *Aligned Archetype*

Like Diddy 'n Biggy baby I won't stop, no I won't stop

Call me a firecracker now you're after all I got

Writin' my very own chapter delete that rapture and that big crock

Of shit, won't quit, you'll see planting my seed I reap and sow

Won't quit, this bitch read palms write songs about all that I know

But see I am not concerned 'bout what I've not learned

I burned it all

*Takeover, **Integration***

You say you love me but want control
I'm not your robot I got a soul,
I do not blame you the theory is old
kept from the women and all the poor
You don't realize how deep it gets
A few in power decide the steps

*Free Up, **Owl Time***

When the weather does change, will your summer last all year round?

Even in the rain I bet we can cast rays and rainbow will be found

*Catch Me, **Integration***

No matter how
much love I get

I'm making freedom
my project

but i promise we must evolve
love is the only way to solve
all the imbalance
i hear the challenge
but we could combine our talents
we could unwind out our talons
all be unblind and balanced
this is the chalice

*Free Up, **Owl Time***

Love your neighbor, do not compare

Labels are over, don't tell me what's fair

Like when you're young, learn how to share

Love like you mean it, without a care

Dance until sunrise, no time to spare

Thought to Thing, **Aligned Archetype**

LETTING GO OF THE SAD GIRL
I DO NOT MOURN HER

INTEGRATING ALL MY SELVES

AND I'M GETTING WARMER

TO THE MASSES I WILL BE
A CELESTIAL INFORMER

LOVE ME, I AM YOUR
CHAMELEON TRANSFORMER

Big Plans, **Aligned Archtype**

A whole spectrum of color surrounds you

*Catch Me, **Integration***

WE ARE WHAT WE SAY WE ARE
WE DEFINE
WE COULD BEND TIME
WE COULD REWIND
WE COULD ERASE
WE COULD EVOLVE
WE COULD REPLACE AND WE COULD SOLVE
ALL THE ISSUES

Divine, *Integration*

But saying I love you ain't easy
in fact some say it's hard

'Cause this is a prison planet
and we are all at large

But the beings have entered
to put the many

Back in charge

L`Outro, *Integration*

Yesterday is not today

I'll let the memories fade away

I gotta keep keep moving on

I had the power all along

Yesterday, **Age of Feminine**

And with the power of Isis I will speak to your

third eye
I'll be your soldier in crisis
I will lick your cheek when you cry

Third Eye, **Aligned Archetype**

Have faith in all your dreams
This world ain't always what it seems
It reflects the negativity
In what we can not guarantee
Be just who you're supposed to be

Let your heart and your soul beam
We all are one, equality
We are alive and so lucky
Feel it, this new energy

Thought to Thing, **Aligned Archetype**

I insist
That what you resist
Will persist

I Insist, ***Aligned Archetype***

So much to do so little time
So much time so little to do
Strike that, reverse it
You like that, rehearse it
Then fight back the curses
From the churches of your rebirthing
You have resurfaced, you are not worthless
You are not tainted, you are not a victim
You aren't the sainted, you have been written
You are the whole, you're every soul
You have a special role

Everything, ***Owl Time***

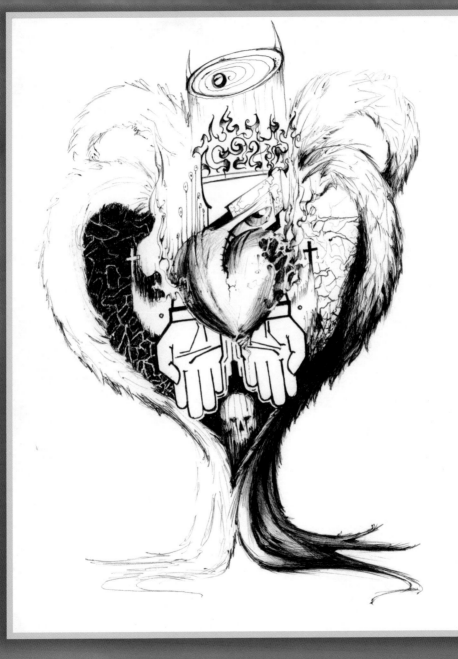

I am steadily building my collection
Of badass women seeking more than perfection
I am just like you
You are my invention
Both sides of the mirror
will create reflection

Say Whatcha Want, **Aligned Archetype**

instead, i'll tell you how i lost my mind
then i got it back
with a soul clap
and om
burn the incense
wake the drone
dial tone get on the phone
spread the word
get in the zone
'cause birds of a feather can flock
thru any weather
and i think it is better if we unite the
tribe 'n do this forever

*Owl Time, **Owl Time***

Just when he thought his life was over
Earth roamer, many legs, one head
Wrapped himself up, over and over
Determined to no longer walk with the dead
Was fairly certain there was nothing left
Encased in curtain took one deep breath
Happenin' to me prolly happenin' to you
I'ma tell li'l story, and I promise that it's true

*Flying Caterpillar, **Owl Time***

Do not be afraid to cry
Soon the tears will surely dry
You have wings and you can fly
There's no limit to your sky

Trapped, *Integration*

I AM THE WATER
YOU ARE THE WATER
WE ARE THE WATER
ALL ARE WATER

Notice the End, **Integration**

I HONOR MY
WORD AS ME
AND I WILL
PUT MYSELF
ON THE TOP
OF MY OWN
TOTEM POLE
I KNOW
MY SOUL
IT WILL NOT
LET ME DROP

*Takeover, **Integration***

We gotta stand up and take what's ours
Show the youth how to reach for the stars

Yesterday, *Age of Feminine*

There's no time for sulking
It's been written and it shall pass
Ascension I am stalking
I'm erasing all of my wrath
Goodbye to my ego
I'm now on the path
My aura is pulsing
My palm shows my map

Say What You Want, **Aligned Archetype**

If you don't start
none then there
won't be none
When you make
your hell then
you cannot run
It's like a secret
seems to have been
kept from
The average person
forgot we're all one

Start None, **Aligned Archtype**

It starts deep inside

we must confide in our higher mind

and build the muscle of ending the hustle

of focusing on peace

of loving all we see

unconditionally, of seeing her in he

*Divine, **Integration***

We can no longer pretend
That we are not one
Rainbow tribe without borders
We must save our sons and our daughters
We must rise above all distorters
Of truth
All ignorers of the root
Cause
That we have not been taught to love without pause
Unconditional
Not provisional
This is pivotal

Free Up, **Owl Time**

Get steady and connect with earth

She will ground you to place of birth

We won't compete, we'll share the turf

Please do not question what you're worth

Mothership, **Aligned Archetype**

I'm the Venus for your Mars
I'm the healing for your scars
I'm the nighttime for your stars
You don't have to look so far

Already Are, *Owl Time*

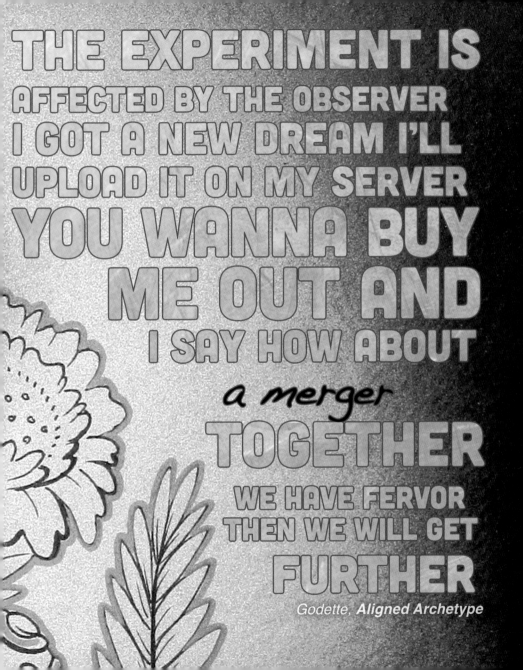

THE EXPERIMENT IS
AFFECTED BY THE OBSERVER
I GOT A NEW DREAM I'LL
UPLOAD IT ON MY SERVER
YOU WANNA BUY
ME OUT AND
I SAY HOW ABOUT
a merger
TOGETHER
WE HAVE FERVOR
THEN WE WILL GET
FURTHER

Godette, *Aligned Archetype*

WHEN I RELEASED MY EXPECTATION
SUDDENLY ALL OF MY RELATIONS ARE FASCINATION

Shadows, Integration

He felt like his species had ruined the earth
He was done crawling and he wanted rebirth
                Saw her encase herself in a womb

Then he asked is there any room
No, so he made his own bed
                to prepare to be dead

But little did he know there was more
                ways that he could grow
And no it didn't mean the end
There was much more he could defend

But not in this form, the demons were inside
Always fed through his greed and pride

He hoped he could
destroy them just in time

*Flying Caterpillar, **Owl Time***

They better have the gemstones ready
Settin' the babies free and our third eye steady
Hand healing is subtle, we touch you
Cells expand no bs to go home with
My aura is thick 'cause I be up in the mix of rapture
Enlightenment, this is what I'm after
The hate got a girl depressed
Wish my ether was an armor to absorb the stress

Revival of the 5th Sun, **Integration**

'CAUSE I COULD
STICK AND MOVE

I am focused
like a soldier

And you've been in my way
heavy like a boulder

AND EVERYBODY'S
SCARED OF DEATH
AND GETTING OLDER

When you release
your fear
come cry

on my
shoulder

*Third Eye, **Aligned Archetype***

Collapse into my quietness
I hope that you do not mind this
Eternal search for my own bliss
When my mind stops playing its tricks

Godette, *Aligned Archetype*

IT'S ALL IN YOU
NOW WHAT WE GONNA DO
HOP IN OUR COCOON
AND SPEAK THROUGH OUR MOON
THE LIGHTS COMING SOON
WE ALL ABOUT TO BLOOM
THERE IS SPACE TO MAKE ROOM
THAT WISH COULD COME TRUE
HEY HEY
PUT YOUR HANDS UP
AND LET ME HEAR YOU SAY
A CATERPILLAR AND A BUTTERFLY HAVE
THE SAME DNA HEY
HEY

Flying Caterpillar, **Owl Time**

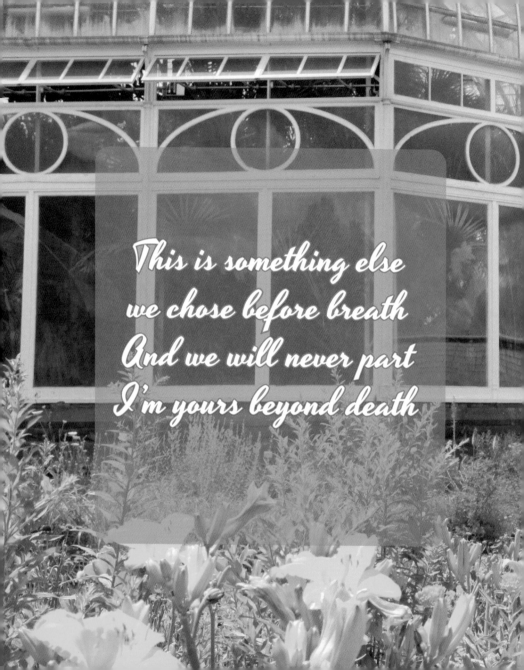

This is something else
we chose before breath
And we will never part
I'm yours beyond death

Signs, Aligned Archetype

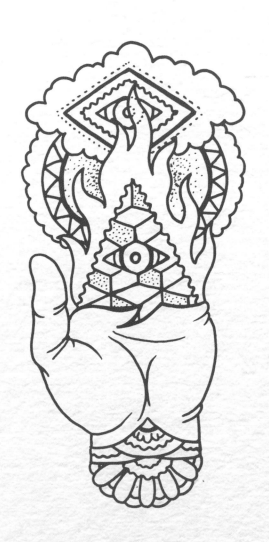

It's fun to some but it's quite wack
People die of what they lack
We get high and spend our cash
Some die without food, you fast
Class is a problem, I see a caste
We create the now in the past
Law of attraction held from grasp
Of those that need to know the path
Creating love dispelling wrath
Master key holders create the facts

Godette, *Aligned Archetype*

Find your inner child.
Release your struggle.
Love everyone and everything.
Be the change you wish to see.

Eleven 11, *Aligned Archetype*

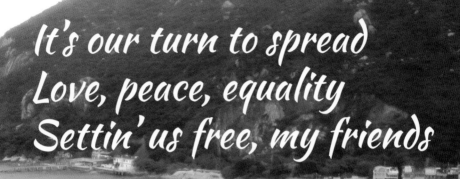

It's our turn to spread
Love, peace, equality
Settin' us free, my friends

*Mad Humans, **Integration***

Ladededadadaday
you can light your own way
Ladededadadaday
today can be your day
Ladededadadaday
I will be lighting my own way
Ladededadadaday
today is my day

*Third Eye, **Aligned Archetype***

City to city, mother to son, and young to old
No need for pity, we are all one, break out this mold
Give back what you stole
Admit it when we lie
It's burying you inside
Be willing to be wrong, stop worryin 'bout looking good
You don't have to be strong
Or hurrying to be what you think you should
You are whole, perfect, strong, powerful
Reflect that in the world and you will live long
Loving, harmonious and happy
It's stunning when all of us are sappy
Full of passion 'n lacking greed
But still human yet perfect indeed
But when we admit our downfall
Suddenly we feel that we belong
To a universal force that holds you up
Keeps you on course
With no remorse

*Mad Humans, **Integration***

Yes, it was finally time to transform
He knew in the babies that were born
A seed to a new way to live
There was more he had to give
I don't know about you
But I can relate
To his state
I have sewn up my case
and I patiently wait
For my wings to erase
All the internal hate

So I can conquer the state
Full of those who are exactly
The same that I chose
Other than name
And other than a body
We are all a story written kinda sloppy
Looking glass is broken
The matrix unplugged, prophecy has been spoken
It's undone
Come up from dungeon
Look up at your sun
Been waiting for a savior
When in fact we are the ones

Flying Caterpillar, **Owl Time**

Now let me leave
you with one final message

Love your enemy and yourself, I am requesting

That we join hands in existential connection

I am you

you are me

there is no discretion

*Notice the End, **Integration***

acknowledgments

I always find it so hard to do acknowledgments for albums and other such projects. My gratitude is so deep and expansive and I fear missing someone as SOOO many people inspire and support. But, here is my best effort and please know that if your name is not here, my gratitude still is.

First and foremost, thanks to Paul, Cathy and Holly at St. Lynn's for giving me such a special opportunity and for believing in the words that spirit has channeled through me. MUCH LOVE!

To my dear friends, Laura for the beautiful pictures, Matt for the captivating art, Brooke for incredible design...if it were not for you I would not have decided to do this project and without you it would be nothing like what I envisioned.

Mom, Aunt Gloria, Grandma, Uncle Mark, Larry, Erin, Aunt Patty, Uncle Jay, Drew, Riss, Maria Cristina, Monique, Stephan, Silvia, Julien and the rest of my family, and my Dad (RIP) – you all are my heart. Joey, I could not ask for a better soul mate; your support and love mean everything to me. Thanks to Victoria, Kathy, Gail, Adrienne, Mary Pat, Regina, Tenanche, and Sheila for mothering my spiritual self and giving me strength. Lani, for all your soul sister support. Leigh, for always being my partner no matter what.

To my fellow Owl Tribe Touring fam...the Wumanity Clan...Mara, Shani, Gemma, Angela, Ana, Caitlin and Jaguar – thank you for the most amazing month of my life during which this book was completed, and thanks for all the healing you brought.

Thanks to my brothers in music. Huggy, Deizel, Josh, Jamal, Chuck Mac, EDan, Jerm, Jason, Ricky, Detonate, Jasiri X, Nice Nate, Emmai,

Gene Stovall, Bonics, Shaun and Alex – thanks for helping me make the music that features these lyrics. Alex D, Nick, and Matt – thank you for giving me visuals beyond this book via video.

To my friends that are family — Roxanne, Marvin, Vanessa, Alana, Kate, Michelle, Erik, Kym, Rod, Nicole, Kaaren, Yolanda, Tasha, Megan, Christine, Chrissy, Sangya, Jeannette, Mel, Meredith, and Katy – thanks for sticking through it all.

I love all of you guys so much. I could write a whole book about how much you mean to me and how much I appreciate your support.

I also must shout out to everyone at my company, Nakturnal. And to Pittsburgh Brewing Company, Verve Wellness, TMWomen.org, Mandi Babkes (holistichealthwithmandi.com), Style Segment, Evolver, OwlTribe.com, everyone at Pittsburgh Landmark Education and Tranformational Alliance Peaceburgh. Magical organizations give magical support. And to Gina Mazza, for writing an amazing book, *Everything Matters, Nothing Matters*, that spawned my connection with St. Lynn's.

Last but certainly not least, my undying gratitude for support from the Owl Tribe – Jodie, Bryan, Sean, Sheleah, Emily, and Christian…without your help this book would not have happened!

Thank you all!

About the Author

Kellee Maize is a rapper, singer, songwriter, dancer and activist from Pittsburgh, Pa. She is also an owner of Nakturnal, an event and online marketing company. Kellee has released three albums and has one on the way, with nearly 1 million total downloads at the time of publishing this book. She is known for writing about all things spiritual. Her music and interests delve into indigenous wisdom, self-development, evolution of consciousness, peace, quantum physics, environmentalism, global issues, extraterrestrial life, yoga and meditation.

www.kelleemaize.com
www.owltribe.com

About the Artists

Laura Petrilla's photography has brought her to wonderful experiences and unique perspectives, allowing her to see people, places and worlds that others rarely see – glimpses of what life truly is. Every year, Laura takes on photography projects outside of her commercial and personal work that create awareness in the world – from empowering women affected by breast cancer, to working with orphanages in Haiti. Her work in this book reflects the many realms that are seen through her lens.

www.misslphotography.com

OCTEEL calls himself "an old soul in the universe, a lover of life." He creates, invents and is inspired by the world around him, both seen and unseen. Whether he's painting drawing or tattooing, his work is often influenced by symbolism, sacred geometry and Native American art. He has participated in art battles, gallery shows, live painting exhibitions, and is available for art commissions. In his free time, he enjoys collecting and growing cactus.

octeel.zenfolio.com